THIS

JOURNAL

BELONGS TO:

_____

DATE:

_____

Trip To:

Dates   From: To:

Where we Stayed:

Overall Score/Rating: ① ② ③ ④ ⑤ ⑥ ⑦ ⑧ ⑨ ⑩

Who we Travelled with:

Places we visited:

What we enjoyed most:

Favorite place(s) to eat:

Places to remember next time:

NOTES / SKETCHES

Trip To: _____

Dates   From: _____   To: _____

Where we Stayed: _____

_____

Overall Score/Rating: ① ② ③ ④ ⑤ ⑥ ⑦ ⑧ ⑨ ⑩

Who we Travelled with: _____

_____

Places we visited: _____

_____

_____

_____

What we enjoyed most: _____

_____

_____

Favorite place(s) to eat: _____

_____

_____

Places to remember next time: _____

_____

_____

NOTES / SKETCHES

_____

_____

_____

_____

_____

_____

_____

_____

_____

_____

_____

Trip To:

Dates   From: To:

Where we Stayed:

Overall Score/Rating: ① ② ③ ④ ⑤ ⑥ ⑦ ⑧ ⑨ ⑩

Who we Travelled with:

Places we visited:

What we enjoyed most:

Favorite place(s) to eat:

Places to remember next time:

NOTES / SKETCHES

Trip To: _____

Dates   From: _____   To: _____

Where we Stayed: _____

_____

Overall Score/Rating: ① ② ③ ④ ⑤ ⑥ ⑦ ⑧ ⑨ ⑩

Who we Travelled with: _____

_____

Places we visited: _____

_____

_____

_____

What we enjoyed most: _____

_____

_____

_____

Favorite place(s) to eat: _____

_____

_____

Places to remember next time: _____

_____

_____

_____

NOTES / SKETCHES

Trip To:

Dates   From: To:

Where we Stayed:

Overall Score/Rating: ① ② ③ ④ ⑤ ⑥ ⑦ ⑧ ⑨ ⑩

Who we Travelled with:

Places we visited:

What we enjoyed most:

Favorite place(s) to eat:

Places to remember next time:

NOTES / SKETCHES

Trip To: _____

Dates   From: _____   To: _____

Where we Stayed: _____

_____

Overall Score/Rating: ① ② ③ ④ ⑤ ⑥ ⑦ ⑧ ⑨ ⑩

Who we Travelled with: _____

_____

Places we visited: _____

_____

_____

_____

What we enjoyed most: _____

_____

_____

Favorite place(s) to eat: _____

_____

_____

Places to remember next time: _____

_____

_____

NOTES / SKETCHES

Trip To:

Dates   From: To:

Where we Stayed:

Overall Score/Rating: ① ② ③ ④ ⑤ ⑥ ⑦ ⑧ ⑨ ⑩

Who we Travelled with:

Places we visited:

What we enjoyed most:

Favorite place(s) to eat:

Places to remember next time:

NOTES / SKETCHES

Trip To: _____

Dates   From: _____ To: _____

Where we Stayed: _____

_____

Overall Score/Rating: ① ② ③ ④ ⑤ ⑥ ⑦ ⑧ ⑨ ⑩

Who we Travelled with: _____

_____

Places we visited: _____

_____

_____

_____

What we enjoyed most: _____

_____

_____

Favorite place(s) to eat: _____

_____

_____

Places to remember next time: _____

_____

_____

NOTES / SKETCHES

Trip To: _____

Dates   From: _____   To: _____

Where we Stayed: _____

_____

Overall Score/Rating: ① ② ③ ④ ⑤ ⑥ ⑦ ⑧ ⑨ ⑩

Who we Travelled with: _____

_____

Places we visited: _____

_____

_____

_____

What we enjoyed most: _____

_____

_____

Favorite place(s) to eat: _____

_____

_____

Places to remember next time: _____

_____

_____

NOTES / SKETCHES

Trip To:

Dates   From: To:

Where we Stayed:

Overall Score/Rating: ① ② ③ ④ ⑤ ⑥ ⑦ ⑧ ⑨ ⑩

Who we Travelled with:

Places we visited:

What we enjoyed most:

Favorite place(s) to eat:

Places to remember next time:

NOTES / SKETCHES

Trip To: _____

Dates   From: _____   To: _____

Where we Stayed: _____

_____

Overall Score/Rating: ① ② ③ ④ ⑤ ⑥ ⑦ ⑧ ⑨ ⑩

Who we Travelled with: _____

_____

Places we visited: _____

_____

_____

_____

What we enjoyed most: _____

_____

_____

Favorite place(s) to eat: _____

_____

_____

Places to remember next time: _____

_____

_____

NOTES / SKETCHES

Trip To: _____

Dates   From: _____   To: _____

Where we Stayed: _____

_____

Overall Score/Rating: ① ② ③ ④ ⑤ ⑥ ⑦ ⑧ ⑨ ⑩

Who we Travelled with: _____

_____

Places we visited: _____

_____

_____

_____

What we enjoyed most: _____

_____

_____

Favorite place(s) to eat: _____

_____

_____

Places to remember next time: _____

_____

_____

NOTES / SKETCHES

Trip To:

Dates   From: To:

Where we Stayed:

Overall Score/Rating: ① ② ③ ④ ⑤ ⑥ ⑦ ⑧ ⑨ ⑩

Who we Travelled with:

Places we visited:

What we enjoyed most:

Favorite place(s) to eat:

Places to remember next time:

NOTES / SKETCHES

Trip To:

Dates   From: To:

Where we Stayed:

Overall Score/Rating: ① ② ③ ④ ⑤ ⑥ ⑦ ⑧ ⑨ ⑩

Who we Travelled with:

Places we visited:

What we enjoyed most:

Favorite place(s) to eat:

Places to remember next time:

NOTES / SKETCHES

Trip To: _____

Dates   From: _____   To: _____

Where we Stayed: _____

_____

Overall Score/Rating: ① ② ③ ④ ⑤ ⑥ ⑦ ⑧ ⑨ ⑩

Who we Travelled with: _____

_____

Places we visited: _____

_____

_____

_____

What we enjoyed most: _____

_____

_____

Favorite place(s) to eat: _____

_____

_____

Places to remember next time: _____

_____

_____

NOTES / SKETCHES

Trip To:

Dates   From: To:

Where we Stayed:

Overall Score/Rating: ① ② ③ ④ ⑤ ⑥ ⑦ ⑧ ⑨ ⑩

Who we Travelled with:

Places we visited:

What we enjoyed most:

Favorite place(s) to eat:

Places to remember next time:

NOTES / SKETCHES

Trip To: _____

Dates   From: _____ To: _____

Where we Stayed: _____

_____

Overall Score/Rating: ① ② ③ ④ ⑤ ⑥ ⑦ ⑧ ⑨ ⑩

Who we Travelled with: _____

_____

Places we visited: _____

_____

_____

_____

What we enjoyed most: _____

_____

_____

Favorite place(s) to eat: _____

_____

_____

Places to remember next time: _____

_____

_____

NOTES / SKETCHES

Trip To: _____

Dates   From: _____   To: _____

Where we Stayed: _____

_____

Overall Score/Rating: ① ② ③ ④ ⑤ ⑥ ⑦ ⑧ ⑨ ⑩

Who we Travelled with: _____

_____

Places we visited: _____

_____

_____

_____

What we enjoyed most: _____

_____

_____

Favorite place(s) to eat: _____

_____

_____

Places to remember next time: _____

_____

_____

_____

NOTES / SKETCHES

Trip To:

Dates   From: To:

Where we Stayed:

Overall Score/Rating: (1) (2) (3) (4) (5) (6) (7) (8) (9) (10)

Who we Travelled with:

Places we visited:

What we enjoyed most:

Favorite place(s) to eat:

Places to remember next time:

NOTES / SKETCHES

Trip To: _____

Dates   From: _____   To: _____

Where we Stayed: _____

_____

Overall Score/Rating: ① ② ③ ④ ⑤ ⑥ ⑦ ⑧ ⑨ ⑩

Who we Travelled with: _____

_____

Places we visited: _____

_____

_____

_____

What we enjoyed most: _____

_____

_____

Favorite place(s) to eat: _____

_____

_____

Places to remember next time: _____

_____

_____

_____

NOTES / SKETCHES

Trip To: _____

Dates   From: _____   To: _____

Where we Stayed: _____

_____

Overall Score/Rating: ① ② ③ ④ ⑤ ⑥ ⑦ ⑧ ⑨ ⑩

Who we Travelled with: _____

_____

Places we Visited: _____

_____

_____

_____

What we enjoyed most: _____

_____

_____

Favorite place(s) to eat: _____

_____

_____

Places to remember next time: _____

_____

_____

NOTES / SKETCHES

Trip To: _____

Dates   From: _____   To: _____

Where we Stayed: _____

_____

Overall Score/Rating: ① ② ③ ④ ⑤ ⑥ ⑦ ⑧ ⑨ ⑩

Who we Travelled with: _____

_____

Places we visited: _____

_____

_____

_____

What we enjoyed most: _____

_____

_____

Favorite place(s) to eat: _____

_____

_____

Places to remember next time: _____

_____

_____

NOTES / SKETCHES

_____

_____

_____

_____

_____

_____

_____

_____

_____

_____

Trip To:

Dates   From: To:

Where we Stayed:

Overall Score/Rating: ① ② ③ ④ ⑤ ⑥ ⑦ ⑧ ⑨ ⑩

Who we Travelled with:

Places we visited:

What we enjoyed most:

Favorite place(s) to eat:

Places to remember next time:

NOTES / SKETCHES

Trip To: _____

Dates   From: _____   To: _____

Where we Stayed: _____

_____

Overall Score/Rating: ① ② ③ ④ ⑤ ⑥ ⑦ ⑧ ⑨ ⑩

Who we Travelled with: _____

_____

Places we visited: _____

_____

_____

_____

What we enjoyed most: _____

_____

_____

Favorite place(s) to eat: _____

_____

_____

Places to remember next time: _____

_____

_____

_____

NOTES / SKETCHES

Trip To:

Dates   From: To:

Where we Stayed:

Overall Score/Rating: ① ② ③ ④ ⑤ ⑥ ⑦ ⑧ ⑨ ⑩

Who we Travelled with:

Places we visited:

What we enjoyed most:

Favorite place(s) to eat:

Places to remember next time:

NOTES / SKETCHES

_____

_____

_____

_____

_____

_____

_____

_____

_____

_____

Trip To: _____

Dates   From: _____   To: _____

Where we Stayed: _____

_____

Overall Score/Rating: ① ② ③ ④ ⑤ ⑥ ⑦ ⑧ ⑨ ⑩

Who we Travelled with: _____

_____

Places we visited: _____

_____

_____

_____

What we enjoyed most: _____

_____

_____

Favorite place(s) to eat: _____

_____

_____

Places to remember next time: _____

_____

_____

_____

NOTES / SKETCHES

Trip To:

Dates   From: To:

Where we Stayed:

Overall Score/Rating: ① ② ③ ④ ⑤ ⑥ ⑦ ⑧ ⑨ ⑩

Who we Travelled with:

Places we visited:

What we enjoyed most:

Favorite place(s) to eat:

Places to remember next time:

NOTES / SKETCHES

Trip To: _____

Dates   From: _____   To: _____

Where we Stayed: _____

_____

Overall Score/Rating: ① ② ③ ④ ⑤ ⑥ ⑦ ⑧ ⑨ ⑩

Who we Travelled with: _____

_____

Places we visited: _____

_____

_____

_____

What we enjoyed most: _____

_____

_____

Favorite place(s) to eat: _____

_____

_____

Places to remember next time: _____

_____

_____

_____

NOTES / SKETCHES

Trip To: _____

Dates   From: _____ To: _____

Where we Stayed: _____
_____

Overall Score/Rating: ① ② ③ ④ ⑤ ⑥ ⑦ ⑧ ⑨ ⑩
_____

Who we Travelled with: _____
_____

Places we visited: _____
_____
_____
_____

What we enjoyed most: _____
_____
_____

Favorite place(s) to eat: _____
_____
_____

Places to remember next time: _____
_____
_____

NOTES / SKETCHES

Trip To: _____

Dates　　　From: _____　　　To: _____

Where we Stayed: _____

_____

Overall Score/Rating: ① ② ③ ④ ⑤ ⑥ ⑦ ⑧ ⑨ ⑩

Who we Travelled with: _____

_____

Places we visited: _____

_____

_____

_____

What we enjoyed most: _____

_____

_____

Favorite place(s) to eat: _____

_____

_____

Places to remember next time: _____

_____

_____

_____

NOTES / SKETCHES

Trip To: _____

Dates   From: _____   To: _____

Where we Stayed: _____

_____

Overall Score/Rating: ① ② ③ ④ ⑤ ⑥ ⑦ ⑧ ⑨ ⑩

Who we Travelled with: _____

_____

Places we visited: _____

_____

_____

_____

What we enjoyed most: _____

_____

_____

_____

Favorite place(s) to eat: _____

_____

_____

Places to remember next time: _____

_____

_____

_____

NOTES / SKETCHES

Trip To: _____

Dates   From: _____ To: _____

Where we Stayed: _____

_____

Overall Score/Rating: ① ② ③ ④ ⑤ ⑥ ⑦ ⑧ ⑨ ⑩

Who we Travelled with: _____

_____

Places we visited: _____

_____

_____

_____

What we enjoyed most: _____

_____

_____

Favorite place(s) to eat: _____

_____

_____

Places to remember next time: _____

_____

_____

_____

NOTES / SKETCHES

Trip To:

Dates   From: To:

Where we Stayed:

Overall Score/Rating: ① ② ③ ④ ⑤ ⑥ ⑦ ⑧ ⑨ ⑩

Who we Travelled with:

Places we visited:

What we enjoyed most:

Favorite place(s) to eat:

Places to remember next time:

NOTES / SKETCHES

Trip To:

Dates   From: To:

Where we Stayed:

Overall Score/Rating: ① ② ③ ④ ⑤ ⑥ ⑦ ⑧ ⑨ ⑩

Who we Travelled with:

Places we visited:

What we enjoyed most:

Favorite place(s) to eat:

Places to remember next time:

NOTES / SKETCHES

Trip To:
_____

Dates   From: To:
_____

Where we Stayed:
_____

_____

Overall Score/Rating: ① ② ③ ④ ⑤ ⑥ ⑦ ⑧ ⑨ ⑩
_____

Who we Travelled with:
_____

_____

Places we visited:
_____

_____

_____

_____

What we enjoyed most:
_____

_____

_____

Favorite place(s) to eat:
_____

_____

_____

Places to remember next time:
_____

_____

_____

NOTES / SKETCHES

Trip To:

Dates   From: To:

Where we Stayed:

Overall Score/Rating: ① ② ③ ④ ⑤ ⑥ ⑦ ⑧ ⑨ ⑩

Who we Travelled with:

Places we visited:

What we enjoyed most:

Favorite place(s) to eat:

Places to remember next time:

NOTES / SKETCHES

Trip To: _____

Dates   From: _____   To: _____

Where we Stayed: _____

_____

Overall Score/Rating: ① ② ③ ④ ⑤ ⑥ ⑦ ⑧ ⑨ ⑩

Who we Travelled with: _____

_____

Places we visited: _____

_____

_____

_____

What we enjoyed most: _____

_____

_____

Favorite place(s) to eat: _____

_____

_____

Places to remember next time: _____

_____

_____

NOTES / SKETCHES

Trip To: _____

Dates   From: _____   To: _____

Where we Stayed: _____
_____

Overall Score/Rating: ① ② ③ ④ ⑤ ⑥ ⑦ ⑧ ⑨ ⑩

Who we Travelled with: _____
_____

Places we visited: _____
_____
_____
_____

What we enjoyed most: _____
_____
_____

Favorite place(s) to eat: _____
_____
_____

Places to remember next time: _____
_____
_____

NOTES / SKETCHES

Trip To: _____

Dates   From: _____   To: _____

Where we Stayed: _____

_____

Overall Score/Rating: ① ② ③ ④ ⑤ ⑥ ⑦ ⑧ ⑨ ⑩

Who we Travelled with: _____

_____

Places we visited: _____

_____

_____

_____

What we enjoyed most: _____

_____

_____

Favorite place(s) to eat: _____

_____

_____

Places to remember next time: _____

_____

_____

_____

NOTES / SKETCHES

Trip To:

Dates   From: To:

Where we Stayed:

Overall Score/Rating: ① ② ③ ④ ⑤ ⑥ ⑦ ⑧ ⑨ ⑩

Who we Travelled with:

Places we visited:

What we enjoyed most:

Favorite place(s) to eat:

Places to remember next time:

NOTES / SKETCHES

_____

_____

_____

_____

_____

_____

_____

_____

_____

_____

_____

Trip To:

Dates   From: To:

Where we Stayed:

Overall Score/Rating: ① ② ③ ④ ⑤ ⑥ ⑦ ⑧ ⑨ ⑩

Who we Travelled with:

Places we visited:

What we enjoyed most:

Favorite place(s) to eat:

Places to remember next time:

NOTES / SKETCHES

Trip To:

Dates   From: To:

Where we Stayed:

Overall Score/Rating: ① ② ③ ④ ⑤ ⑥ ⑦ ⑧ ⑨ ⑩

Who we Travelled with:

Places we visited:

What we enjoyed most:

Favorite place(s) to eat:

Places to remember next time:

NOTES / SKETCHES

Trip To: _____

Dates   From: _____   To: _____

Where we Stayed: _____
_____

Overall Score/Rating: ① ② ③ ④ ⑤ ⑥ ⑦ ⑧ ⑨ ⑩

Who we Travelled with: _____
_____

Places we visited: _____
_____
_____
_____

What we enjoyed most: _____
_____
_____

Favorite place(s) to eat: _____
_____
_____

Places to remember next time: _____
_____
_____
_____

NOTES / SKETCHES

Trip To: _____

Dates   From: _____   To: _____

Where we Stayed: _____

_____

Overall Score/Rating: ① ② ③ ④ ⑤ ⑥ ⑦ ⑧ ⑨ ⑩

Who we Travelled with: _____

_____

Places we visited: _____

_____

_____

_____

What we enjoyed most: _____

_____

_____

Favorite place(s) to eat: _____

_____

_____

Places to remember next time: _____

_____

_____

_____

NOTES / SKETCHES

Trip To:

Dates   From: To:

Where we Stayed:

Overall Score/Rating: ① ② ③ ④ ⑤ ⑥ ⑦ ⑧ ⑨ ⑩

Who we Travelled with:

Places we visited:

What we enjoyed most:

Favorite place(s) to eat:

Places to remember next time:

NOTES / SKETCHES

Trip To:

Dates   From: To:

Where we Stayed:

Overall Score/Rating: ① ② ③ ④ ⑤ ⑥ ⑦ ⑧ ⑨ ⑩

Who we Travelled with:

Places we visited:

What we enjoyed most:

Favorite place(s) to eat:

Places to remember next time:

NOTES / SKETCHES

Trip To:

Dates From: To:

Where we Stayed:

Overall Score/Rating: ① ② ③ ④ ⑤ ⑥ ⑦ ⑧ ⑨ ⑩

Who we Travelled with:

Places we visited:

What we enjoyed most:

Favorite place(s) to eat:

Places to remember next time:

NOTES / SKETCHES

Trip To: _____

Dates   From: _____   To: _____

Where we Stayed: _____

_____

Overall Score/Rating: ① ② ③ ④ ⑤ ⑥ ⑦ ⑧ ⑨ ⑩

Who we Travelled with: _____

_____

Places we visited: _____

_____

_____

_____

What we enjoyed most: _____

_____

_____

Favorite place(s) to eat: _____

_____

_____

Places to remember next time: _____

_____

_____

NOTES / SKETCHES

Trip To:

Dates   From: To:

Where we Stayed:

Overall Score/Rating: ① ② ③ ④ ⑤ ⑥ ⑦ ⑧ ⑨ ⑩

Who we Travelled with:

Places we visited:

What we enjoyed most:

Favorite place(s) to eat:

Places to remember next time:

NOTES / SKETCHES

Trip To: _____

Dates   From: _____   To: _____

Where we Stayed: _____
_____

Overall Score/Rating: ① ② ③ ④ ⑤ ⑥ ⑦ ⑧ ⑨ ⑩

Who we Travelled with: _____
_____

Places we visited: _____
_____
_____
_____

What we enjoyed most: _____
_____
_____

Favorite place(s) to eat: _____
_____
_____

Places to remember next time: _____
_____
_____

NOTES / SKETCHES

Trip To:

Dates   From: To:

Where we Stayed:

Overall Score/Rating: ① ② ③ ④ ⑤ ⑥ ⑦ ⑧ ⑨ ⑩

Who we Travelled with:

Places we visited:

What we enjoyed most:

Favorite place(s) to eat:

Places to remember next time:

NOTES / SKETCHES

_____

_____

_____

_____

_____

_____

_____

_____

_____

_____

_____

Trip To:

Dates   From: To:

Where we Stayed:

Overall Score/Rating: ① ② ③ ④ ⑤ ⑥ ⑦ ⑧ ⑨ ⑩

Who we Travelled with:

Places we visited:

What we enjoyed most:

Favorite place(s) to eat:

Places to remember next time:

NOTES / SKETCHES

Trip To: _____

Dates   From: _____   To: _____

Where we Stayed: _____
_____

Overall Score/Rating: ① ② ③ ④ ⑤ ⑥ ⑦ ⑧ ⑨ ⑩

Who we Travelled with: _____
_____

Places we visited: _____
_____
_____
_____

What we enjoyed most: _____
_____
_____

Favorite place(s) to eat: _____
_____
_____

Places to remember next time: _____
_____
_____
_____

NOTES / SKETCHES

Trip To:

Dates   From: To:

Where we Stayed:

Overall Score/Rating: ① ② ③ ④ ⑤ ⑥ ⑦ ⑧ ⑨ ⑩

Who we Travelled with:

Places we visited:

What we enjoyed most:

Favorite place(s) to eat:

Places to remember next time:

NOTES / SKETCHES

Trip To:

Dates   From: To:

Where we Stayed:

Overall Score/Rating: ① ② ③ ④ ⑤ ⑥ ⑦ ⑧ ⑨ ⑩

Who we Travelled with:

Places we visited:

What we enjoyed most:

Favorite place (s) to eat:

Places to remember next time:

Made in United States
Troutdale, OR
12/15/2023

15913212R00066